# The Armor of God for Your Daily Battles
## Ephesians 6:10-18

### Spiritual Protection from Spiritual Attacks

*Pastor Jeremy Markle*

## Walking in the WORD Ministries

Pastor Jeremy Markle
www.walkinginthewordministries.net

*The Armor of God for Your Daily Battles*
*Ephesians 6:10-18*

*Spiritual Protection*
*from*
*Spiritual Attacks*

Unless otherwise noted,
all Scripture quotations are from the King James Version.

Published by Walking in the WORD Ministries
www.walkinginthewordministries.net

Printed in the United States of America

ISBN: 978-0692561324

# Content

# Content

# Ephesians 6:10-18

Finally, my brethren,
be strong in the Lord, and in the power of his might.
Put on the whole armour of God,
that ye may be able to stand
against the wiles of the devil.
For we wrestle not against flesh and blood,
but against principalities, against powers,
against the rulers of the darkness of this world,
against spiritual wickedness in high places.
Wherefore take unto you
the whole armour of God,
that ye may be able to withstand in the evil day,
and having done all, to stand.
Stand therefore,
having your loins girt about with truth,
and having on the breastplate of righteousness;
And your feet shod
with the preparation of the gospel of peace;
Above all, taking the shield of faith,
wherewith ye shall be able to quench
all the fiery darts of the wicked.
And take the helmet of salvation,
and the sword of the Spirit,
which is the word of God:
Praying always with all prayer
and supplication in the Spirit,
and watching thereunto
with all perseverance
and supplication
for all saints;

## II Timothy 2:3-4

Thou therefore endure hardness,
as a good soldier of Jesus Christ.
No man that warreth entangleth himself
with the affairs of this life;
that he may please him
who hath chosen him to be a soldier.

## II Timothy 4:6-8

For I am now ready to be offered,
and the time of my departure is at hand.
I have fought a good fight,
I have finished my course,
I have kept the faith:
Henceforth there is laid up for
me a crown of righteousness,
which the Lord, the righteous judge,
shall give me at that day:
and not to me only,
but unto all them also
that love his appearing.

# Prologue

**II Timothy 3:16-17**
*All scripture is given by inspiration of God,*
*and is profitable for doctrine,*
*for reproof, for correction,*
*for instruction in righteousness:*
*That the man of God may be perfect,*
*throughly furnished unto all good works.*

God has made His plan and purpose clear. He has personally inspired the Bible to accomplish specific tasks for the benefit of each believer. He desires that each believer enjoys a spiritual life which is *"perfect"* or mature, and which produces *"good works"* or right actions. For this reason, He clearly states that His Word has four jobs: He has given man His written Word, *"for doctrine, for reproof, for correction, for instruction in righteousenss."* *"Doctrine"* simply represents information and teaching of truth. *"Reproof"* is the process by which the doctrine or teaching is compared to ones life to find where sin has occurred. *"Correction"* provides the opportunity to repent of and change those areas of sin in order to seek a right relationship with God. *"Instruction in Righteousness"* is the provision of protection from sin in the future by providing warnings and truth-based instruction which will guide the obedient believer away from falling into the traps of sin in the future.

Now, armed with a brief understanding of the plan and purpose of the Word of God in the life of each believer, I invite you to search the Scriptures to understand more of what God says about the spiritual battles you are facing and will face, and how God desires you to gain the victory by asking these four questions:

1. **What does the Bible say about ...?**
2. **In what areas of your life have you not been ...?**
3. **What must you confess and change in your life, ...?**
4. **What teaching about ... can help you live in obedience from this moment forward?**

# Strength for the Battle

## Ephesians 6:10
*Finally, my brethren,*
*be strong in the Lord,*
*and in the power of his might.*

A soldier in a physical battle understands that if his strength fails, he will fall prey to the enemy even if he has an unlimited supply of weapons. Strength is the key to clear thinking and swift action. The same is true for a believer. He must have spiritual strength to be victorious. He must depend on the spiritual nourishment provided by God and depend on Him to ultimately win the battle.

Take some time each day to discover more about your personal weaknesses and the limitless source of strength you have available when you depend on God.

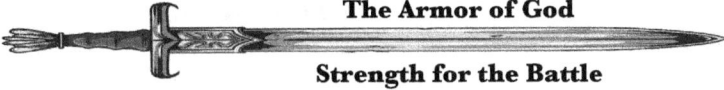

# Day # 1
## Romans 5:1-2, 6-9

**What does the Bible say about** your condition before salvation?

_____

_____

_____

**In what areas of your life have you not been** remembering and appreciating the strength of Christ given to you in your salvation?

_____

_____

_____

**What must you confess and change in your life,** so that you can remember and apply the strength of your salvation?

_____

_____

_____

**What teaching about** God's strength for you beginning at salvation **can help you live in obedience from this moment forward**?

_____

_____

_____

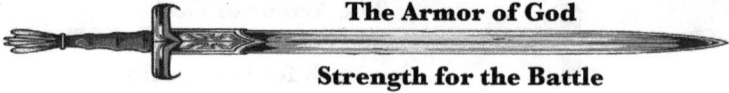

# Day # 2
# John 15:1-8

**What does the Bible say about** the source of a believer's strength?

_____

_____

_____

**In what areas of your life have you not been** depending on the Lord for His strength?

_____

_____

_____

**What must you confess and change in your life,** so that you can correctly depend upon the Lord?

_____

_____

_____

**What teaching about** God's strength for you when you depend on Him **can help you live in obedience from this moment forward**?

_____

_____

_____

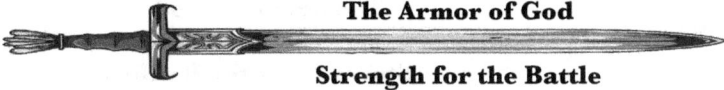

# Day # 3
# I Peter 5:10-11
# *II Corinthians 12:7-10*

**What does the Bible say about** God's grace for you in your time of difficultly? *Who should receive the glory in the end?*

_____

_____

_____

**In what areas of your life have you not been** trusting God's grace to help you through your difficulty?

_____

_____

_____

**What must you confess and change in your life,** so that you glorify God during and after your difficulty?

_____

_____

_____

**What teaching about** God's grace for your strength **can help you live in obedience from this moment forward**?

_____

_____

_____

## Day # 4
## II Corinthians 3:4-5, 4:7-10

**What does the Bible say about** a believer's source of strength to minister for God?

_____

_____

_____

**In what areas of your life have you not been** depending in God's strength to accomplish your responsibilities?

_____

_____

_____

**What must you confess and change in your life,** so that you are properly depending in God to accomplish each task?

_____

_____

_____

**What teaching about** God's strength for each of your tasks **can help you live in obedience from this moment forward**?

_____

_____

_____

# Day # 5
## Isaiah 40:28-31, 41:10

**What does the Bible say about** the strength of the Lord for those who "wait" or eagerly look to Him?

_____

_____

_____

**In what areas of your life have you not been** "waiting" on the Lord?

_____

_____

_____

**What must you confess and change in your life,** so that you are more expectant upon the Lord for His prevision of strength?

_____

_____

_____

**What teaching about** God's strength for you when you "wait" on Him **can help you live in obedience from this moment forward**?

_____

_____

_____

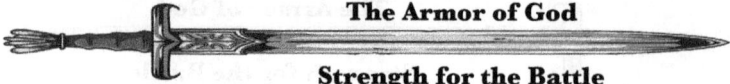

# Day # 6
# Matthew 26:40-41
# *Ephesians 3:14-21, Philippians 4:6-7*

**What does the Bible say about** prayer which is necessary in order for a believer to have spiritual strength? *What area of the believer's life is often weak and prevents this exercise?*

_____

_____

_____

**In what areas of your life have you not been** exercising your prayer life and receiving the blessing of God's strength?

_____

_____

**What must you confess and change in your life,** so that you are exercising your prayer life correctly and enjoying the strength it provides?

_____

_____

**What teaching about** God's strength provided to you through prayer **can help you live in obedience from this moment forward**?

_____

_____

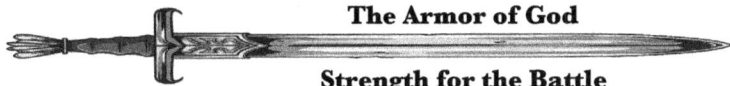

## Day # 7
## Review

### Philippians 4:13
### *I can do all things through Christ*
### *which strengtheneth me.*

1.  Romans 5:1-2, 6-9 - In what condition are you without Jesus Christ?

    _____

2.  John 15:1-8 - What must you do to produce spiritual fruit?

    _____

3.  I Peter 5:10-11 - Based on God's grace for you in times of trouble, what does He want you to be?

    _____

4.  II Corinthians 3:4-5, 4:7-10 - Who must you depend on to help you accomplish each task in your life?

    _____

5.  Isaiah 40:28-31, 41:10 - What has God promised will not happen to you if you "wait" on Him?

    _____

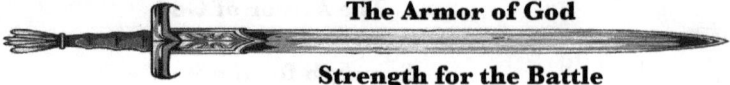

6.  Matthew 26:40-41, *Ephesians 3:14-21, Philippians 4:6-7* - What must be a part of your life if you are going to enjoy God's strength?

    _____

7.  Philippians 4:13 - Who is your strength?

    _____

# The Enemy in the Battle

**Ephesians 6:11-12**
*Put on the whole armour of God,*
*that ye may be able to stand against*
*the wiles of the devil.*
*For we wrestle not against flesh and blood,*
*but against principalities, against powers,*
*against the rulers of the darkness*
*of this world,*
*against spiritual wickedness in high places.*

A good soldier searches to find information about his enemy. He looks for his strengths, weaknesses, and his tactics, and he tries to understand his objective. The same is true for a soldier of the cross. He must know as much as possible about his enemy, Satan. He must be aware of the types of spiritual attacks he will face on a daily basis.

Take some time each day to discover more about your spiritual enemy, so that you can better defend yourself when he attacks.

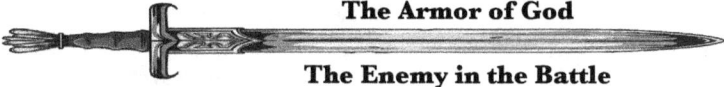

# Day # 1
# Isaiah 14:12-17

**What does the Bible say about** Satan and his downfall?

_____

_____

_____

**In what areas of your life have you not been** protecting yourself from your own personal pride?

_____

_____

_____

**What must you confess and change in your life,** so that you do not experience the same damage of pride Satan experienced?

_____

_____

_____

**What teaching about** Satan's pride **can help you live in obedience from this moment forward**?

_____

_____

_____

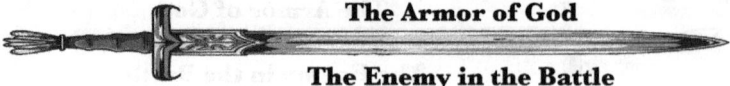

# Day # 2
# John 8:43-45
# *Ephesians 2:1-3*

**What does the Bible say about** Satan and those who follow him?

_____

_____

_____

**In what areas of your life have you not been** protecting yourself from the lusts and lies of Satan?

_____

_____

_____

**What must you confess and change in your life,** so that your life is not affected by Satan's lusts and lies?

_____

_____

_____

**What teaching about** Satan and his followers which **can help you live in obedience from this moment forward**?

_____

_____

_____

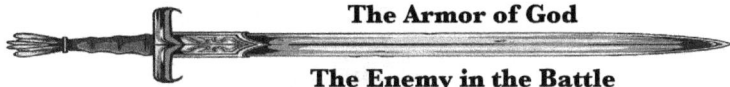

# Day # 3
## Ephesians 4:26-27

**What does the Bible say about** Satan having room in your life?

_____

_____

_____

**In what areas of your life have you not been** careful with your anger and permitted Satan to have control?

_____

_____

_____

**What must you confess and change in your life,** so that Satan does not cause damage any longer?

_____

_____

_____

**What teaching about** Satan and anger **can help you live in obedience from this moment forward**?

_____

_____

_____

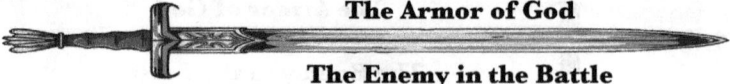

# Day # 4
# James 4:6-8

**What does the Bible say about** how you can resist Satan?

_____

_____

_____

**In what areas of your life have you not been** resisting Satan?

_____

_____

_____

**What must you confess and change in your life,** so that Satan will flee from you?

_____

_____

_____

**What teaching about** resisting Satan **can help you live in obedience from this moment forward**?

_____

_____

_____

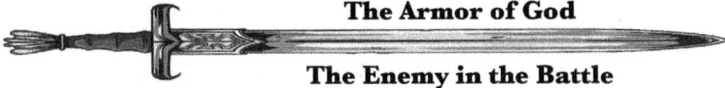

## Day # 5
## I Peter 5:8-9

**What does the Bible say about** Satan's desire to destroy you?

_____

_____

_____

**In what areas of your life have you not been** careful of Satan's attacks?

_____

_____

_____

**What must you confess and change in your life,** so that you are resisting Satan?

_____

_____

_____

**What teaching about** how to resist Satan **can help you live in obedience from this moment forward**?

_____

_____

_____

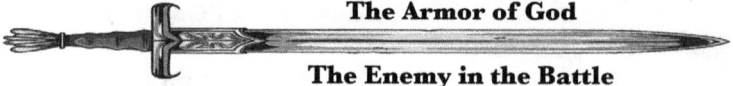

# Day # 6
# Revelation 12:7-11

**What does the Bible say about** Satan's work against you?

_____

_____

_____

**In what areas of your life have you not been** protected from the accusations of Satan?

_____

_____

_____

**What must you confess and change in your life,** so that Satan does not have room to accuse you of sin?

_____

_____

_____

**What teaching about** Satan's accusations and destruction **can help you live in obedience from this moment forward**?

_____

_____

_____

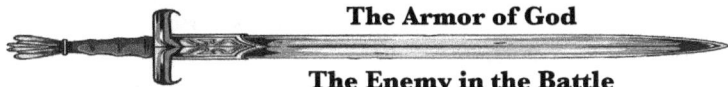

# Day # 7
# Review

## II Corinthians 11:14
*And no marvel;*
*for Satan himself*
*is transformed into an angel of light.*

1.  Isaiah 14:12-17 - What caused Satan's downfall?

    _____

2.  John 8:43-45, Ephesians 2:1-3 - Satan is the father of what, and who follows him?

    _____

3.  Ephesians 4:26-27 - What provides room for Satan to have influence in your life?

    _____

4.  James 4:6-8 - What must you do to resist Satan?

    _____

5.  I Peter 5:8-9 - What does Satan desire to do to you?

    _____

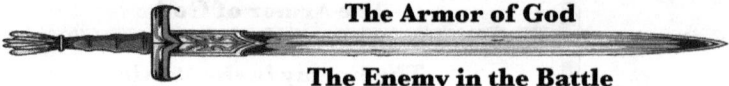

6.      Revelation 12:7-11 - What does Satan do to you and about you?

_____

7.      II Corinthians 11:14 - Like what does Satan attempt to appear?

_____

# Standing in the Battle

**Ephesians 6:13**
*Wherefore take unto you
the whole armour of God,
that ye may be able to withstand
in the evil day,
and having done all, to stand.*

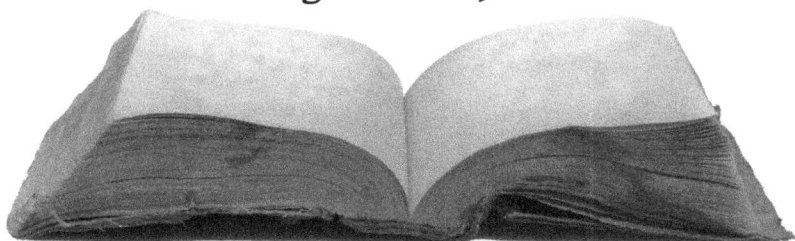

The soldier who is not solidly grounded in his physical position can be knocked down quickly. The same is true in the spiritual battle. It is important that each believer is secure in his relationship with God and is stable is his purpose of life, so that the enemy can not overtake him.

Take some time each day to discover more about the importance of being well grounded in your spiritual life.

# Day # 1
## Luke 6:47-49
## *Psalm 1:1-6*

**What does the Bible say about** those who listen to and obey the teaching of Christ?

_____

_____

_____

**In what areas of your life have you not been** listening to and obeying the teaching of Christ?

_____

_____

_____

**What must you confess and change in your life,** so that you can enjoy stability in life?

_____

_____

_____

**What teaching about** the teaching of Christ **can help you live in obedience from this moment forward**?

_____

_____

_____

# Day # 2
# I Corinthians 15:58

**What does the Bible say about** being steadfast?

_____
_____
_____

**In what areas of your life have you not been** steadfast?

_____
_____
_____

**What must you confess and change in your life,** so that you can be steadfast?

_____
_____
_____

**What teaching about** steadfastness **can help you live in obedience from this moment forward**?

_____
_____
_____

# Day # 3
## Colosenses 1:21-23, 2:6-7

**What does the Bible say about** continuing in the faith?

_____

_____

_____

**In what areas of your life have you not been** continuing in the faith?

_____

_____

_____

**What must you confess and change in your life,** so that you can be in the faith?

_____

_____

_____

**What teaching about** continuing in the faith **can help you live in obedience from this moment forward**?

_____

_____

_____

# Day # 4
## Philippians 1:25-28

**What does the Bible say about** standing in unity?

_____

_____

_____

**In what areas of your life have you not been** standing in unity?

_____

_____

_____

**What must you confess and change in your life,** so that you can stand in unity with other believers?

_____

_____

_____

**What teaching about** standing in unity **can help you live in obedience from this moment forward**?

_____

_____

_____

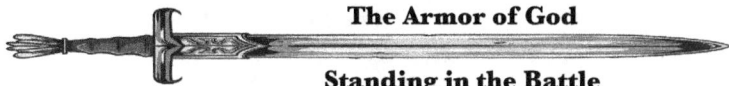

# Day # 5
## II Timothy 2:3-4

**What does the Bible say about** enduring as a good soldier?

_____

_____

_____

**In what areas of your life have you not been** enduring as a good soldier?

_____

_____

_____

**What must you confess and change in your life,** so that you can be enduring?

_____

_____

_____

**What teaching about** enduring **can help you live in obedience from this moment forward**?

_____

_____

_____

# Day # 6
## I Corinthians 2:1-5

**What does the Bible say about** the stability of your faith? *Where should it come from?*

_____

_____

_____

**In what areas of your life have you not been** stable in your faith?

_____

_____

_____

**What must you confess and change in your life,** so that you can be stable in your faith?

_____

_____

_____

**What teaching about** the stability of your faith **can help you live in obedience from this moment forward**?

_____

_____

_____

# Day # 7
# Review

## I Corinthians 16:13
### *Watch ye, stand fast in the faith, quit you like men, be strong.*

1.  Luke 6:47-49, Psalms 1:1-6 - How can you ensure that you will be spiritually stable?

   _____

2.  I Corinthians 15:58 - What must you always be doing in the Lord's work?

   _____

3.  Colossians 1:21-23, 2:6-7 - What is the foundation of your faith?

   _____

4.  Philippians 1:25-28 - How should we stand with other believers?

   _____

5.  II Timothy 2:3-4 - How must a you maintain yourself so that you are a good soldier for God?

   _____

6.   I Corinthians 2:1-5 - Teaching based upon Whose wisdom will provide you stability?

   _____

7.   II Corinthians 16:13 - What must you stand fast in if you are to be a stable believer?

   _____

# The Armor for the Battle
## *The Belt*
### The Unity of Truth

**Ephesians 6:14**
***Stand therefore,***
***having your loins girt about with truth ...***

A key element to a soldier's armor is his belt. Without his belt, all his other armor becomes disconnected and falls to the ground, becoming a source of stumbling, rather than a source of protection. In the believer's life, the same is true. If there is a lack of consistent honesty and a rejection of falsehood throughout every area of life, all of the other areas of an individual's life will fall apart due to distrust and inconsistency.

Take some time each day to discover more about the need for truth to be a part of every area of our spiritual life.

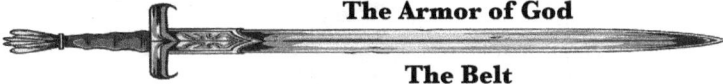

**The Belt**
*The Unity of Truth*

# Day # 1
# Psalm 51:6-12

**What does the Bible say about** truth in your private life?

_____

_____

_____

**In what areas of your life have you not been** guarding truth in your private life?

_____

_____

_____

**What must you confess and change in your life,** so that you can have truth in your private life?

_____

_____

_____

**What teaching about** truth in your personal life **can help you live in obedience from this moment forward**?

_____

_____

_____

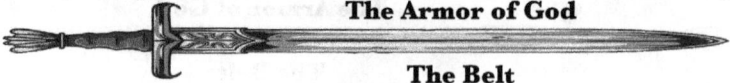

# Day # 2
# John 8:31-32

**What does the Bible say about** knowing the truth?

_____

_____

_____

**In what areas of your life have you not been** knowing
and applying to the truth?

_____

_____

_____

**What must you confess and change in your life,** so
that you know and apply the truth?

_____

_____

_____

**What teaching about** knowing and applying the truth
from Jesus Christ **can help you live in obedience from
this moment forward**?

_____

_____

_____

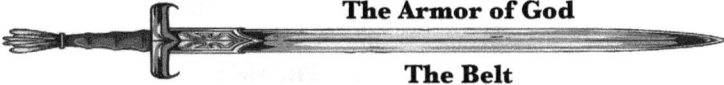

# Day # 3
# John 16:7-15
# *John 17:17*

**What does the Bible say about** your personal Guide to knowing truth?

_____

_____

_____

**In what areas of your life have you not been** guided by the Holy Spirit?

_____

_____

_____

**What must you confess and change in your life,** so that you are guided by truth?

_____

_____

_____

**What teaching about** the Holy Spirit's guidance in truth **can help you live in obedience from this moment forward**?

_____

_____

_____

**The Belt**
*The Unity of Truth*

# Day # 4
# I John 1:1-10

**What does the Bible say about** walking in the truth?

_____

_____

_____

**In what areas of your life have you not been** walking in the truth?

_____

_____

_____

**What must you confess and change in your life,** so that you can walk in the truth?

_____

_____

_____

**What teaching about** walking in the truth **can help you live in obedience from this moment forward**?

_____

_____

_____

# Day # 5
# Ephesians 4:15, 25

**What does the Bible say about** speaking the truth?

_____

_____

_____

**In what areas of your life have you not been** speaking the truth in love?

_____

_____

_____

**What must you confess and change in your life,** so that your speak the truth in love?

_____

_____

_____

**What teaching about** speaking the truth in love **can help you live in obedience from this moment forward**?

_____

_____

_____

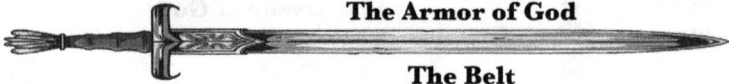

**The Belt**
*The Unity of Truth*

# Day # 6
## I John 3:14-18

**What does the Bible say about** love and truth?

_____

_____

_____

**In what areas of your life have you not been** loving others in truth?

_____

_____

_____

**What must you confess and change in your life,** so that you can truly love others?

_____

_____

_____

**What teaching about** loving in truth **can help you live in obedience from this moment forward**?

_____

_____

_____

**The Belt**
*The Unity of Truth*

# Day # 7
# Review

## Proverbs 23:23
*Buy the truth, and sell it not;*
*also wisdom, and instruction,*
*and understanding.*

1. Psalm 51:6-12 - Where does God want truth to begin in your life?

   _____

2. John 8:31-32 - Who must you follow in order to know truth?

   _____

3. John 16:7-15, John 17:17 - Who will guide you into truth through the Word of God?

   _____

4. I John 1:1-10 - When are you walking in truth?

   _____

5. Ephesians 4:15, 25 - How should you speak?

   _____

6. I John 3:14-18 - How does love operate?

   _____

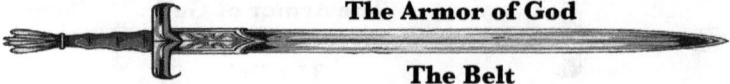

7.      Proverbs 23:23 - For what should you be willing
to spend money?

_____

# The Armor for the Battle
## *The Breastplate*
### The Protection of Righteousness

**Ephesians 6:14**
*... and having on
the breastplate of righteousness;*

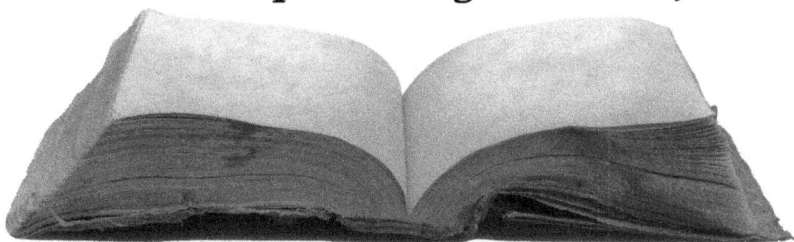

A breastplate is like a bullet-proof vest. Its purpose is to protect the vital organs of the soldier. For a believer, righteousness, or right living, protects the spiritual vital organs. Without right living a believer falls prey to the destruction of his spiritual life because of his sin.

Take some time each day to discover more about the need for righteousness/right living to be a part every area of your spiritual life.

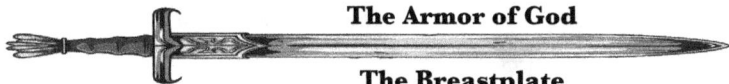

**The Breastplate**
*The Protection of Righteousness*

# Day # 1
# II Corinthians 6:14-18

**What does the Bible say about** mixing righteousness with unrighteousness?

_____

_____

_____

**In what areas of your life have you not been** separating yourself from unrighteousness?

_____

_____

_____

**What must you confess and change in your life,** so that you are separated from unrighteousness?

_____

_____

_____

**What teaching about** living separated from unrighteousness **can help you live in obedience from this moment forward**?

_____

_____

_____

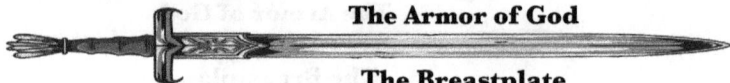

**The Breastplate**
*The Protection of Righteousness*

# Day # 2
# Philippians 1:8-11

**What does the Bible say about** the fruit of righteousness? *Who is the source of the fruit for righteousness in your life?*

_____

_____

_____

**In what areas of your life have you not been** full of righteous fruit?

_____

_____

_____

**What must you confess and change in your life,** so that you produce righteous fruit?

_____

_____

_____

**What teaching about** the fruit of righteousness **can help you live in obedience from this moment forward**?

_____

_____

_____

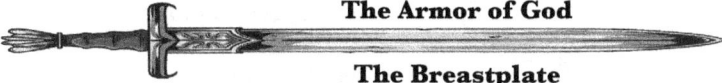

**The Breastplate**
*The Protection of Righteousness*

# Day # 3
# Hebrews 12:5-13

**What does the Bible say about** the correction of God in the production of the fruit of righteousness?

_____

_____

_____

**In what areas of your life have you not been** permitting God to produce the fruit of righteousness?

_____

_____

_____

**What must you confess and change in your life,** so that you can produce the fruit of righteousness?

_____

_____

_____

**What teaching about** correction of God for the fruit of righteousness **can help you live in obedience from this moment forward**?

_____

_____

_____

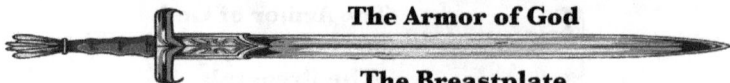

# Day # 4
# Romans 6:11-23

**What does the Bible say about** serving righteousness?

_____

_____

_____

**In what areas of your life have you not been** serving righteousness?

_____

_____

_____

**What must you confess and change in your life,** so that you are serving righteousness?

_____

_____

_____

**What teaching about** serving righteousness **can help you live in obedience from this moment forward**?

_____

_____

_____

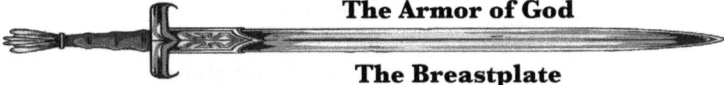

**The Breastplate**
*The Protection of Righteousness*

# Day # 5
# I Peter 2:19-24

**What does the Bible say about** how you should live while suffering for righteousness?

_____

_____

_____

**In what areas of your life have you not been** living patiently like Christ when suffering for righteousness?

_____

_____

_____

**What must you confess and change in your life** so that you are patient when suffering for righteousness?

_____

_____

_____

**What teaching about** being patient while suffering for righteousness **can help you live in obedience from this moment forward**?

_____

_____

_____

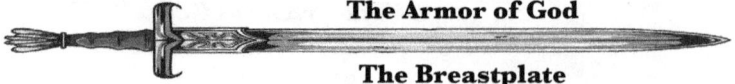

**The Breastplate**
*The Protection of Righteousness*

# Day # 6
## Psalm 18:20-24, 92:1-15 (12-15)

**What does the Bible say about** the result of a righteous life?

_____

_____

_____

**In what areas of your life have you not been** enjoying the results of a righteous life?

_____

_____

_____

**What must you confess and change in your life,** so that you can enjoy the results of a righteous life?

_____

_____

_____

**What teaching about** the results of a righteous life **can help you live in obedience from this moment forward**?

_____

_____

_____

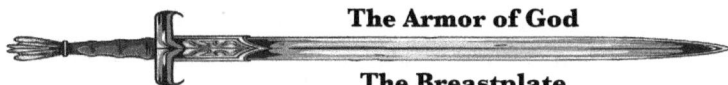

# Day # 7
# Review

## I Corinthians 15:34
*Awake to righteousness, and sin not;*
*for some have not the knowledge of God:*
*I speak this to your shame.*

1.   II Corinthians 6:14-18 - What does God want you to stay away from?

   _____

2.   Philippians 1:8-11 - Who will produce righteousness in your life?

   _____

3.   Hebrews 12:5-13 - What is the purpose of God's correction when you are in sin?

   _____

4.   Romans 6:11-23 - What is the result of serving righteousness?

   _____

5.   I Peter 2:19-24 - How should you display your dependence in God when you suffer for righteousness?

   _____

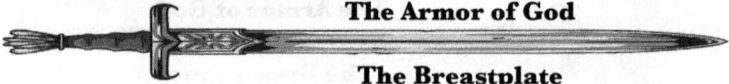

6.  Psalms 18:20-24, 92:1-15 (13-15) - What is the reward of a righteous life?

    _____

7.  I Corinthians 15:34 - What is the opposite of righteousness?

    _____

# The Armor for the Battle
## *The Shoes*
### The Power of the Gospel

**Ephesians 6:15**
*And your feet shod*
*with the preparation of the gospel of peace;*

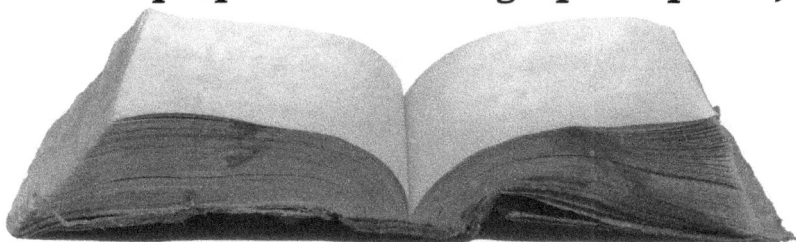

A soldier's boots are very important. Without proper footwear, a soldier cannot stand firm or advance forward with power. A believer is to have the Gospel as his footwear. The Gospel must be seen as the foundation for the Christian life, as well as the very motivating factor to keep moving forward. A believer must be sure that his spiritual boots are firmly attached and that they are fulfilling their purpose.

Take some time each day to discover more about the need for Gospel of peace to be a part of every area of our spiritual life.

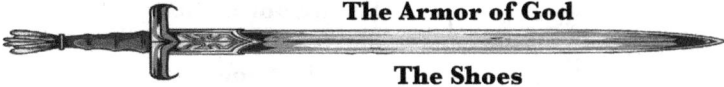

# Day # 1
## Romans 1:16-17
### *I Corinthians 15:1-4*

**What does the Bible say about** power of the Gospel?

_____

_____

_____

**In what areas of your life have you not been** communicating according to the power of the Gospel?

_____

_____

_____

**What must you confess and change in your life,** so that you are communicating the power of the Gospel?

_____

_____

_____

**What teaching about** the power of the Gospel **can help you live in obedience from this moment forward**?

_____

_____

_____

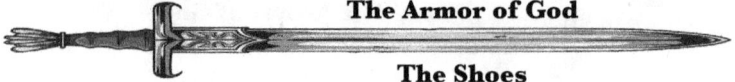

# Day # 2
# II Corinthians 4:1-6

**What does the Bible say about** the Gospel being hid?

_____

_____

_____

**In what areas of your life have you not been** displaying the Gospel?

_____

_____

_____

**What must you confess and change in your life,** so that you are displaying the Gospel?

_____

_____

_____

**What teaching about** the Gospel being hid **can help you live in obedience from this moment forward**?

_____

_____

_____

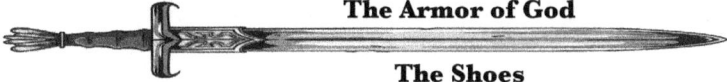

# Day # 3
# Galatians 1:6-12

**What does the Bible say about** any other gospel (other than salvation by faith in Jesus Christ)?

_____

_____

_____

**In what areas of your life have you not been** rejecting any other gospel (religion)?

_____

_____

_____

**What must you confess and change in your life,** so that no other gospel has an influence?

_____

_____

_____

**What teaching about** the true Gospel of Jesus Christ **can help you live in obedience from this moment forward**?

_____

_____

_____

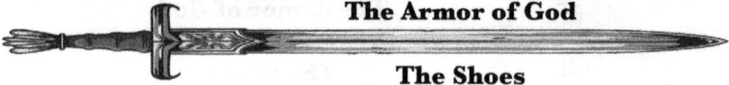

# Day # 4
# Matthew 28:18-20
# *Mark 16:15-16*

**What does the Bible say about** to whom you should preach (tell) the Gospel?

_____

_____

_____

**In what areas of your life have you not been** preaching the Gospel to all those who need to hear it?

_____

_____

_____

**What must you confess and change in your life,** so that you can preach the Gospel to all those who need to hear it?

_____

_____

_____

**What teaching about** preaching the Gospel **can help you live in obedience from this moment forward**?

_____

_____

_____

# Day # 5
# Romans 10:13-15

**What does the Bible say about** God's plan for preaching the Gospel?

_____

_____

_____

**In what areas of your life have you not been** a part of God's plan for preaching the Gospel?

_____

_____

_____

**What must you confess and change in your life,** so that you are a part of God's plan for preaching the Gospel?

_____

_____

_____

**What teaching about** God's plan for preaching the Gospel **can help you live in obedience from this moment forward**?

_____

_____

_____

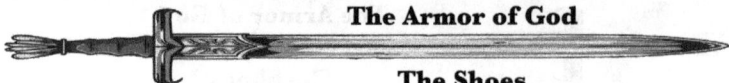

# Day # 6
# Ephesians 6:18-20
## *Acts 4:29-31*

**What does the Bible say about** boldness in sharing the Gospel?

_____

_____

_____

**In what areas of your life have you not been** boldly sharing the Gospel?

_____

_____

_____

**What must you confess and change in your life,** so that you boldly share the Gospel?

_____

_____

_____

**What teaching about** boldness in sharing the Gospel **can help you live in obedience from this moment forward**?

_____

_____

_____

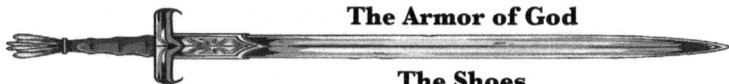

**The Shoes**
*The Power of the Gospel*

# Day # 7
# Review

## I Thessalonians 1:5
*For our gospel came not unto you
in word only,
but also in power, and in the Holy Ghost,
and in much assurance;
as ye know what manner of men we were
among you for your sake.*

1.  Romans 1:16-17 - What does the Gospel have the power to do?

    _____

2.  II Corinthians 4:1-6 - What should never happen to the light of the Gospel?

    _____

3.  Galatians 1:6-12 - What must you do to any "gospel" that is not the true Gospel of Jesus Christ?

    _____

4.  Matthew 28:18-20, Mark 16:15-16 - What should you do with the Gospel?

    _____

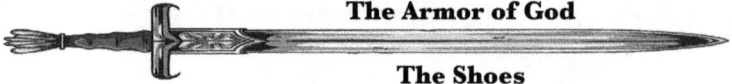

5.     Romans 10:13-15 - What is God's plan for how the Gospel is to be spread?

_____

6.     Ephesians 6:18-20, Acts 4:29-31 - What should you pray for as you share the Gospel?

_____

7.     I Thessalonians 1:5 - In what three ways should you display the Gospel as you share it in your words?

_____
_____
_____

# The Armor for the Battle
## *The Shield*
### The Protection of Faith

**Ephesians 6:16**
***Above all, taking the shield of faith,
wherewith ye shall be able to quench
all the fiery darts of the wicked.***

Often times, a good soldier will find something to shield him from the enemy's attacks. He will wisely seek out tactical positions which prevent the enemy's bullets from wounding him. For a spiritual soldier, faith is his shield. As Satan attacks with darts of trails, temptations, etc., to cause doubt as to God's goodness and provision, faith protects the believer from being spiritually wounded with discouragement and taken out of the battle.

Take some time each day to discover more about the need for faith to be a part of every area of our spiritual life.

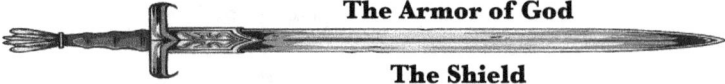

# Day # 1
# Hebrews 11:1, 6

**What does the Bible say about** faith in God?

_____

_____

_____

**In what areas of your life have you not been** living in faith in God?

_____

_____

_____

**What must you confess and change in your life,** so that you maintain faith in God?

_____

_____

_____

**What teaching about** faith in God **can help you live in obedience from this moment forward**?

_____

_____

_____

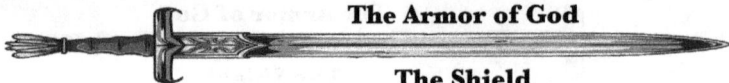

# Day # 2
## Colosenses 1:19-23

**What does the Bible say about** the result of you being grounded in the faith?

_____

_____

_____

**In what areas of your life have you not been** grounded in the faith?

_____

_____

_____

**What must you confess and change in your life,** so that you are grounded in the faith?

_____

_____

_____

**What teaching about** being grounded in the faith **can help you live in obedience from this moment forward**?

_____

_____

_____

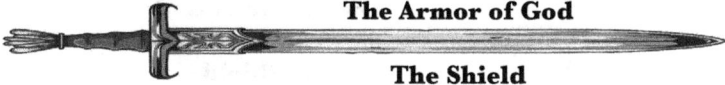

**The Shield**
*The Protection of Faith*

# Day # 3
# I John 5:4-5
# *I Peter 5:8-9*

**What does the Bible say about** gaining spiritual victory?

_____

_____

_____

**In what areas of your life have you not been** gaining spiritual victory?

_____

_____

_____

**What must you confess and change in your life,** so that you can gain spiritual victory?

_____

_____

_____

**What teaching about** spiritual victory **can help you live in obedience from this moment forward**?

_____

_____

_____

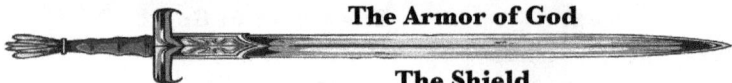

# Day # 4
# James 2:14-26

**What does the Bible say about** the works of faith?

_____

_____

_____

**In what areas of your life have you not been** putting your faith to work?

_____

_____

_____

**What must you confess and change in your life,** so that your faith is shown by your works?

_____

_____

_____

**What teaching about** the works of faith **can help you live in obedience from this moment forward**?

_____

_____

_____

**The Shield**
*The Protection of Faith*

# Day # 5
# James 1:5-8
# *Mark 11:22-24*

**What does the Bible say about** praying in faith?

_____

_____

_____

**In what areas of your life have you not been** praying in faith?

_____

_____

_____

**What must you confess and change in your life,** so that you start praying in faith?

_____

_____

_____

**What teaching about** praying in faith **can help you live in obedience from this moment forward**?

_____

_____

_____

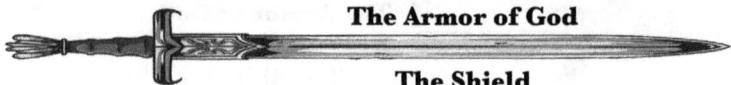

## Day # 6
## Hebrews 12:1-3

**What does the Bible say about** eliminating any distractions from your faith in Jesus Christ?

_____

_____

_____

**In what areas of your life have you not been** focused correctly in your faith in Jesus Christ?

_____

_____

_____

**What must you confess and change in your life,** so that your are not distracted from your faith in Jesus Christ?

_____

_____

_____

**What teaching about** not being distracted from faith in Jesus Christ **can help you live in obedience from this moment forward**?

_____

_____

_____

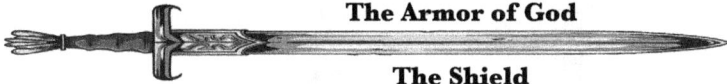

# Day # 7
# Review

## Romans 10:17
### *So then faith cometh by hearing, and hearing by the word of God.*

1.  Hebrews 11:1, 6 - In whom must you put our faith?

    _____

2.  Colossians 1:19-23 - What is the result of a grounded faith?

    _____

3.  I John 5:4-5, *I Peter 5:8-9* - How can you gain victory over the world?

    _____

4.  James 2:14-16 - What should your faith be producing?

    _____

5.  James 1:5-8, *Mark 11:22-24* - How should you pray to God?

    _____

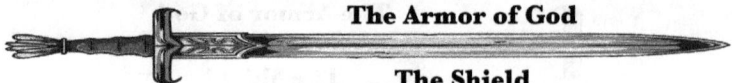

6.  Hebrews 12:1-3 - What must be removed from your life so that you maintain proper faith?

    _____

7.  Romans 10:17 - How can you grow in your faith?

    _____

# The Armor for the Battle
## *The Helmet*
### The Clarity of Thought Based on Salvation

### Ephesians 6:17
### *And take the helmet of salvation ...*

One of the most vulnerable parts of a soldier's body is his head. It also is the most important. Without proper thinking, the soldier cannot control the rest of his body to fulfill his assignment. For this reason, a good soldier will take special care to always use his helmet. A spiritual soldier must take the same care. He must always remember his salvation and the new life God has provided for him. He must take charge of his thinking and never allow himself to be distracted in the battle.

Take some time each day to discover more about the need for the truths of salvation to be a part of every area of your spiritual life.

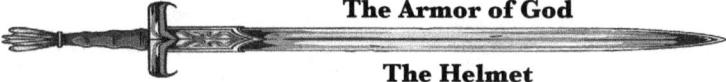

# Day # 1
# Philippians 2:12-16

**What does the Bible say about** living (working) out your salvation?

_____

_____

_____

**In what areas of your life have you not been** living out your salvation?

_____

_____

_____

**What must you confess and change in your life,** so that you can live out your salvation?

_____

_____

_____

**What teaching about** living out your salvation **can help you live in obedience from this moment forward**?

_____

_____

_____

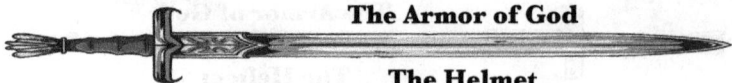

**The Helmet**
*The Clarity of Thought Based on Salvation*

# Day # 2
# Romans 13:11-14

**What does the Bible say about** your spiritual alertness based on your salvation?

_____

_____

_____

**In what areas of your life have you not been** spiritually alert?

_____

_____

_____

**What must you confess and change in your life,** so that you are spiritually alert?

_____

_____

_____

**What teaching about** spiritual alertness **can help you live in obedience from this moment forward**?

_____

_____

_____

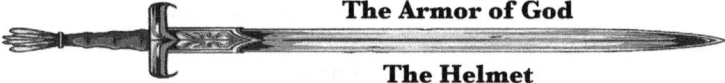

**The Helmet**
*The Clarity of Thought Based on Salvation*

# Day # 3
## Colosenses 1:19-23

**What does the Bible say about** the result of being secure in our salvation?

_____

_____

_____

**In what areas of your life have you not been** living based upon the security of your salvation?

_____

_____

_____

**What must you confess and change in your life,** so that you are living in the security of your salvation?

_____

_____

_____

**What teaching about** the security of your salvation **can help you live in obedience from this moment forward**?

_____

_____

_____

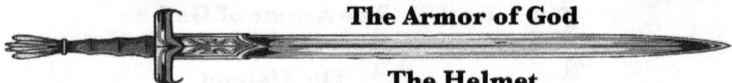

# Day # 4
# Ephesians 4:17-32

**What does the Bible say about** changing your thinking (mind)?

_____

_____

_____

**In what areas of your life have you not been** changing your thinking (thinking like the new man)?

_____

_____

_____

**What must you confess and change in your life,** to begin thinking correctly?

_____

_____

_____

**What teaching about** changing your thinking **can help you live in obedience from this moment forward**?

_____

_____

_____

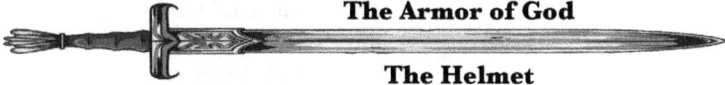

# Day # 5
# Titus 2:11-14

**What does the Bible say about** the teaching from salvation?

_____

_____

_____

**In what areas of your life have you not been** following the teaching from salvation?

_____

_____

_____

**What must you confess and change in your life,** so that you are following the teaching from salvation?

_____

_____

_____

**What teaching about** salvation **can help you live in obedience from this moment forward**?

_____

_____

_____

# Day # 6
# Colosenses 2:5-10

**What does the Bible say about** your walk (lifestyle) based on your salvation?

_____

_____

_____

**In what areas of your life have you not been** walking according to your salvation?

_____

_____

_____

**What must you confess and change in your life,** so that you are walking according to your salvation?

_____

_____

_____

**What teaching about** your walk in accordance to your salvation **can help you live in obedience from this moment forward**?

_____

_____

_____

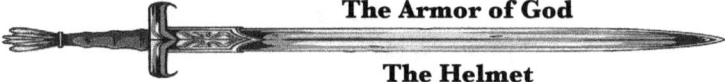

# Day # 7
# Review

## I John 2:5-6
*But whoso keepeth his word,*
*in him verily is the love of God perfected:*
*hereby know we that we are in him.*
*He that saith he abideth in him*
*ought himself also so to walk,*
*even as he walked.*

1.  Philippians 2:12-16 - How is salvation worked out (lived out)?

    _____

2.  Romans 13:11-14 - How does spiritual alertness help you live?

    _____

3.  Colossians 1:19-23 - How are we secure in our salvation?

    _____

4.  Ephesians 4:17-32 - How should your thinking be different than from before you were saved?

    _____

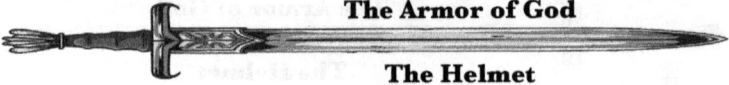

5.    Titus 2:11-14 - How should your salvation teach you to live?

_____

6.    Colossians 2:5-10 - How should you walk (live) after your salvation?

_____

7.    I John 2:5-6 - What does following Jesus' example show about your life?

_____

# The Armor for the Battle
## *The Sword*
### The Weapon of Protection and Penetration

**Ephesians 6:17**
*... and the sword of the Spirit,*
*which is the word of God:*

A soldier who carries a sword or knife knows that he can gain the advantage if he knows his weapon well. The sword or knife can be used to defend the blows of others, as well as be used to put a stop to the attacker, but only if it is used with precision. The Word of God is the believer's sword. It too can provide great protection and deliver fatal blows to the enemy when the spiritual soldier is regularly receiving training and consistently practices what he has learned.

Take some time each day to discover more about the need for the Word of God in every area of your spiritual life.

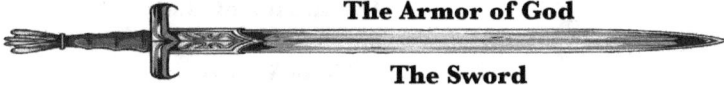

**The Sword**
*The Weapon of Protection and Penetration*

# Day # 1
# Hebrews 4:12

**What does the Bible say about** the strength of the Bible?

_____

_____

_____

**In what areas of your life have you not been** permitting the Bible's strength to work in your life?

_____

_____

_____

**What must you confess and change in your life,** so that you can experience the Bible's strength?

_____

_____

_____

**What teaching about** the Bible's strength **can help you live in obedience from this moment forward**?

_____

_____

_____

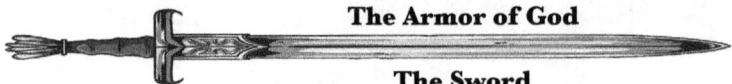

## Day # 2
## Psalm 119:9-11

**What does the Bible say about** the cleansing of the Bible?

_____

_____

_____

**In what areas of your life have you not been** cleansing yourself with the Bible?

_____

_____

_____

**What must you confess and change in your life,** so that you can experience the Bible's cleansing?

_____

_____

_____

**What teaching about** the Bible's cleansing **can help you live in obedience from this moment forward**?

_____

_____

_____

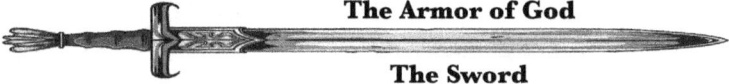

**The Sword**
*The Weapon of Protection and Penetration*

# Day # 3
# II Timothy 2:15, 3:14-17

**What does the Bible say about** studying the Bible?

_____

_____

_____

**In what areas of your life have you not been** studying the Bible?

_____

_____

_____

**What must you confess and change in your life,** so that you do study the Bible?

_____

_____

_____

**What teaching about** studying the Bible **can help you live in obedience from this moment forward**?

_____

_____

_____

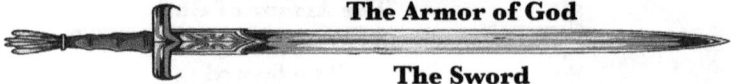

**The Sword**
*The Weapon of Protection and Penetration*

# Day # 4
# Psalm 19:7-11

**What does the Bible say about** the work of the Bible?

_____

_____

_____

**In what areas of your life have you not been** allowing the Bible to work in your life?

_____

_____

_____

**What must you confess and change in your life,** so that the Bible can complete its work?

_____

_____

_____

**What teaching about** work of the Bible **can help you live in obedience from this moment forward**?

_____

_____

_____

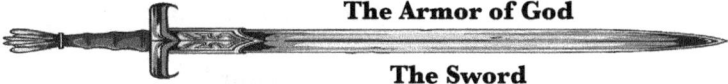

# Day # 5
# Psalm 1:1-6

**What does the Bible say about** the blessing of thinking (meditating) on the Bible?

_____

_____

_____

**In what areas of your life have you not been** thinking on the Bible?

_____

_____

_____

**What must you confess and change in your life,** so that you are thinking on the Bible?

_____

_____

_____

**What teaching about** thinking about the Bible **can help you live in obedience from this moment forward**?

_____

_____

_____

**The Sword**
*The Weapon of Protection and Penetration*

# Day # 6
# James 1:22-25

**What does the Bible say about** obeying the Bible?

_____

_____

_____

**In what areas of your life have you not been** obeying the Bible?

_____

_____

_____

**What must you confess and change in your life,** so that you are obeying the Bible?

_____

_____

_____

**What teaching about** obeying the Bible **can help you live in obedience from this moment forward**?

_____

_____

_____

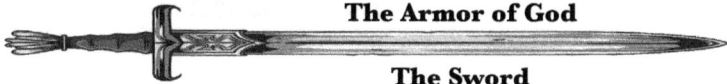

# Day # 7
# Review

## I Peter 2:2
*Desead, como niños recién nacidos,*
*la leche espiritual no adulterada,*
*para que por ella crezcáis para salvación,*

1.   Hebrews 4:12 - What type of strength does the Bible have?

   _____

2.   Psalm 119:9-11 - How can the Bible cleanse you spiritually?

   _____

3.   II Timothy 2:15, 3:14-17 - What must you do with the Bible?

   _____

4.   Psalm 19:7-11 - What type of work does the Bible accomplish?

   _____

5.   Psalm 1:1-6 - What will you be if you meditate (think) on the Bible?

   _____

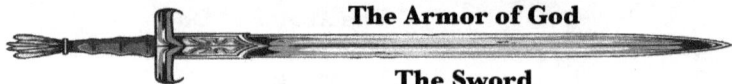

6.    James 1:22-25 - What must you do after you read or hear the Bible?

_____

7.    I Peter 2:2 - What will help you to grow spiritually?

_____

# Constant Communication in the Battle

**Ephesians 6:18**
*Praying always
with all prayer and supplication
in the Spirit,
and watching thereunto
with all perseverance and supplication
for all saints;*

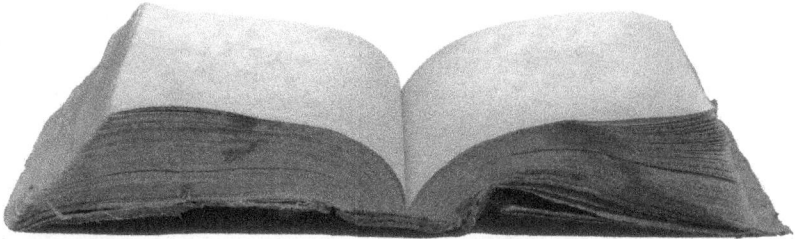

A modern-day soldier has many resources to keep him in touch with his superiors: radio, phone, Internet, satellite, etc. He realizes that communication is of the utmost importance if he will gain the victory. When he lacks communication, he increases the probability for confusion, lack of supplies, lack of direction, etc. The spiritual soldier has the same need for communication. His "device" for communication with the Commander and Chief is prayer. Although there are times when his communication is disrupted due to his failure, he knows that at any time and in any circumstance, he can once again reconnect with God through prayer and once agaim gain, be back in the battle where he belongs.

Take some time each day to discover more about the need for prayer in every area of your spiritual life.

# Day # 1
# Matthew 6:5-15

**What does the Bible say about** praying correctly (the how and what) according to the example of Jesus Christ?

_____

_____

_____

**In what areas of your life have you not been** praying correctly?

_____

_____

_____

**What must you confess and change in your life,** so that you can pray correctly?

_____

_____

_____

**What teaching about** praying correctly **can help you live in obedience from this moment forward**?

_____

_____

_____

# Day # 2
## Luke 11:5-13

**What does the Bible say about** you praying to God for your needs?

_____

_____

_____

**In what areas of your life have you not been** praying correctly to God for your needs?

_____

_____

_____

**What must you confess and change in your life,** so that you are praying correctly to God for your needs?

_____

_____

_____

**What teaching about** praying to God for your needs **can help you live in obedience from this moment forward**?

_____

_____

_____

# Day # 3
## Romans 8:26-27

**What does the Bible say about** the help of the Holy Spirit during prayer?

_____

_____

_____

**In what areas of your life have you not been** depending upon the help of the Holy Spirit during prayer?

_____

_____

_____

**What must you confess and change in your life,** so that you are experiencing the help of the Holy Spirit during prayer?

_____

_____

_____

**What teaching about** the help of the Holy Spirit **can help you live in obedience from this moment forward**?

_____

_____

_____

## Day # 4
## James 4:1-3
## *Psalm 37:4-5*

**What does the Bible say about** why you do not have what you desire?

_____
_____
_____

**In what areas of your life have you not been** receiving the desires of your heart?

_____
_____
_____

**What must you confess and change in your life,** so that you can see your desires provided?

_____
_____
_____

**What teaching about** receiving your desires **can help you live in obedience from this moment forward**?

_____
_____
_____

# Day # 5
## I John 3:22-24, 5:14-15

**What does the Bible say about** the need for obedience to have your prayers answered?

_____

_____

_____

**In what areas of your life have you not been** having your prayers answered because of a lack of obedience?

_____

_____

_____

**What must you confess and change in your life,** so that you can experience answered prayer?

_____

_____

_____

**What teaching about** obedience and prayer **can help you live in obedience from this moment forward**?

_____

_____

_____

# Day # 6
## Ephesians 3:10-21

**What does the Bible say about** praying for others?

_____

_____

_____

**In what areas of your life have you not been** praying for others?

_____

_____

_____

**What must you confess and change in your life,** so that you are praying for others?

_____

_____

_____

**What teaching about** praying for others **can help you live in obedience from this moment forward**?

_____

_____

_____

## Day # 7
## Review

**Philippians 4:6-7**
*Be careful for nothing;*
*but in every thing by prayer*
*and supplication with thanksgiving*
*let your requests be made known unto God.*
*And the peace of God,*
*which passeth all understanding,*
*shall keep your hearts and minds*
*through Christ Jesus.*

1.  Matthew 6:5-15 - To Whom and for what should you prayer?

    _____

    _____

2.  Luke 11:5-13 - Does God want to answer your prayer?

    _____

3.  Romans 8:26-27 - Who will help you pray?

    _____

4.  James 4:1-3 - When will you receive the desires of your heart?

    _____

5.  I John 3:22-24, 5:14-15 - What must you do in order to have answered prayer?

    _____

6.  Ephesians 3:10-21 - Who should you prayer for?

    _____

7.  Philippians 4:6-7 - What should you pray for?

    _____

# Other Ministry Resources Available
# From
# Walking in the WORD Ministries

*Marriage: A Covenant Before God* presents 10 biblical studies about marriage, each one is based on the marital relationship of Adam and Eve and has the purpose of helping young couples understand God's plan and purpose for their life together. Included are practical questions, illustrations, and applications for each biblical truth in order that the couple might grow in their knowledge of each other and how they can glorify God together.

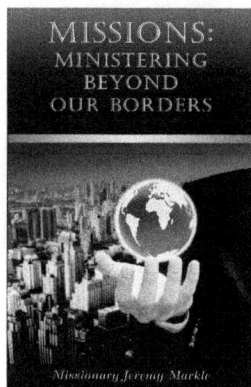

*Missions: Ministering Beyond Our Borders* was written to provide insight into the physical, emotional, and spiritual adjustments a missionary faces as he begins his new life and ministry. Throughout its pages you will find spiritual encouragements for the missionary and helpful hints for his family and friends who desire to support him in his service to their Lord and Savior Jesus Christ. There is also a "Missionary Edition," which provides a large appendix with additional tips specifically for missionaries.

*The Deputation Trail: Ministry or a Means to an End?* was written to help missionaries during their pre-field ministry by presenting biblically-based philosophies and practical tips to guide them through a God-honoring, church-expanding, and believer-edifying, deputation ministry.